The Ships We Sail

Modern Fables for the Unfinished Soul

JANET HELEN FIX

First edition 2025
Published in Canton, GA, USA by thewordverve
(www.thewordverve.com)

eBook ISBN: 978-1-956856-95-8
Paperback ISBN: 978-1-956856-96-5
Hardback ISBN: 978-1-956856-97-2

Library of Congress Control Number: 2025943202

Cover art designed by Elena Stowell
www.elenastowell.com

Interior illustrations created by the author using DALL·E 3 AI

Cover and interior design by Robin Krauss at Linden Design
www.lindendesign.biz

eBook formatting by thewordverve

TABLE OF CONTENTS

TO MY FELLOW TRAVELERS

Fables have long been used to teach—lessons tucked into fur and feather, tree and tide. But these stories are a little different. They aren't warnings or answers. They're reminders.

Some of these fables may offer you comfort. Others may stir something you forgot you were holding. You may see yourself in the red fox, the oak tree, or the quiet spider with her unsent letter. And if you don't? That's okay too.

These aren't stories that insist. They don't teach in straight lines. Some of them even contradict each other—on purpose. Because life is not one fixed path. There are seasons for becoming, and seasons

for undoing. Times to hold firm, and times to let go. Even truth sometimes shifts depending on the light.

So take what feels true. Let the rest drift away like a ship that's already sailed.

You are not expected to read these all at once. In fact, I hope you don't. These stories are short, but they were never meant to be rushed. Let them find you. Let them sit with you. Let them echo. And if just one lingers—truly lingers—I hope it brings you back to yourself.

With love and light on your journey,

Janet

CHAPTER 1

THE FOX AND THE EMPTY BUNDLE

(For those learning to let go without forgetting)

In a quiet season between what was and what will be, a red fox carried an empty bundle.

The cloth was soft with age, stitched from days long past. It had once held treasures: small paws of those who needed her, wildflowers offered by little ones, songs hummed in the dark. The bundle had been full of life and laughter and purpose.

But now, it was light. Almost too light. The ones Fox had carried had grown, walked ahead, woven lives of their own. And still, she carried it—out of

habit, out of love, out of not knowing what else to
hold.

Fox wandered the familiar woods, tracing old
paths. She curled up in places that once brought
comfort but found they no longer fit. Her heart
ached, not from sorrow exactly, but from the
emptiness that comes when your hands remember
a weight that's no longer there.

For a long time, she thought something was wrong with her. That she should have moved on by now. That she should be full of new dreams, running faster, reaching farther.

But one morning, as dawn broke gently through the trees, she stopped.

She looked not at the bundle, but at the road ahead. And for the first time, she wondered what she might want to carry next—not for someone else, but for herself.

Carefully, reverently, she opened the bundle and placed a single thing inside: a small, carved stone from the river, smoothed by time. It was quiet, beautiful, hers.

She smiled her foxy smile.

She took her first step forward. Not to forget the past, but to walk with it beside her, never behind..

❧ MORAL ☙

Letting go is not forgetting.
It's making space for what's next.

CHAPTER 2

THE WHALE WHO HELD TOO MUCH

*(For those who swallow sorrow
just to keep the peace)*

She was one of the great giants of the ocean but moved with quiet grace.

No one ever asked how it felt to carry so much.

Whale swallowed everything: tears no one cried, secrets no one told, and anger no one dared to speak aloud. Grief, abandonment, shame . . . they all sank into her, seeping into skin and tissue, organ and bone.

She thought if she held it long enough, it would eventually dissolve. Disappear. Like sugar in warm water.

But it didn't, of course. These were the things that stuck hard and fast and changed a being.

So, the weight grew heavy in her bones. Her whale song became silent. And the ocean inside her roared louder than the one around her. And she wept, defeated.

Until one day, the sun stroked her body through the water's surface. Whale had felt it before, long ago, but this time, something was different. She realized it was the only pleasure she had felt in a long time. And now she wondered why she always swam so deep, coming up only for air, then moving back down again. Heavy. Stuck. This time, she rose closer to the surface. There was no rage in her, no protest from her weighted body. She only felt a release.

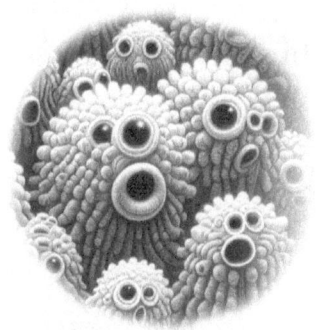

She breached the surface, and with her whole being, she sang. A sound so ancient and low it woke coral from sleep and made distant boats pause.

The song wasn't her best, really. It wasn't soft. But it was honest.

The sorrow spilled out of her, all the burdens she'd carried for so long, not in pieces, but in waves.

Other whales came. They didn't ask questions or inspect her or judge her. They didn't try to fix her. They just joined the song. Why had she hidden for so long? Why had she not sung and danced? These things that would lighten her—why had she not done them?

When it ended, the water felt lighter, and she too, in it.

Not because the burdens were completely gone, but because it had been witnessed and shared. Because she had danced. Because she had sung.

 MORAL

Healing begins not when the sorrow disappears,
but when it is sung.

CHAPTER 3

THE TREE THAT WASN'T A WILLOW

(For those who stand strong, not just for themselves, but for others)

They called her Willow... because she bent. She smiled when it hurt. She stayed when she wanted to run.

She made it look easy to survive the storm without breaking.

And so, they called her graceful. Delicate. Soothing.

She wore the name like a ribbon and let the wind take her voice. But in her roots, down where no one saw, she knew she wasn't a willow at all.

She was Oak. Wide and wild-hearted. Knotted with knowing. Scarred from battles she hadn't even known she was a part of until they were over.

And she was beautiful—her branches thick and sturdy. Her roots deep and substantial in the earth. Her leaves changing with the seasons, offering food and shade to those who needed it. And in the winter she would rest, to prepare for other seasons. The legacy of her abundance.

She didn't simply want to sway. She wanted to stand, strong and glorious. To hold birds in her arms and not apologize for being solid and resolute in her knowing.

One day, a terrible storm came, as they some-times did. A hard one, mean with rain . . . the kind that tests one's name.

The willows around her bowed. They bent, and they swayed. The strained against the storm's force.

But this time, she didn't do any of that. She stayed still. And the storm broke around her. Not through her. Not under her.

Around her.

They called her stubborn after that. But she smiled, slow and sure. Because it was never about what they called her. It was about what she knew.

She had never been Willow. She was Oak, some-thing ancient and rooted and true.

❧ MORAL ☙

When you are true to your roots—your soul line—
your strength becomes a refuge for others.

CHAPTER 4

THE TURTLE WHO GREW WILDFLOWERS IN HIS WOUNDS

(For those who bear their scars like secrets)

e was good at hiding. Hiding the scars and cracks and sorrows beneath a quiet shell and a steady gait. No one saw the breaking. His back was hard, his eyes calm, his path unwavering.

Turtle knew how to keep things in.

When he was young, they said:

"Be strong."

"Keep going."

"Don't cry."

And he didn't. Not once. He held grief like a sacred breath—quiet, heavy, and unshared.

Until one day, the wounds he'd hidden began to bloom. Not bleed. Not break.

Bloom.

First from beneath his shell. Then along his limbs. Then from the soft skin under his jaw and the places no one ever thought to look.

Wildflowers and mosses, born not from seeds and spores, but from bruises and the soil of unspoken pain.

He tried to hide them—scraping them gently

against stones, retreating further into his shell. He walked more slowly and sought smaller paths.

But still they grew until others began to notice. Some stared, some whispered. He couldn't hide his wounds anymore. And he shook with uncertainty and fear of facing what he'd tried so hard to bury.

One morning, a gentle voice came from above, soft and unexpected. "These are beautiful. Oh, what you must have endured to grow them."

Trembling, the turtle looked up to see a majestic stag standing there, its antlers as wide as the sky.

Stag knelt, dipped its head, and brushed its velvet antlers gently along the turtle's mossy edge. "What are they called?"

Turtle didn't know. He had never named his grief, the things that hurt him. But he began to speak, not to explain the pain so much, but to honor the wounds that had nurtured the blooms. Other animals appeared, acknowledging his stories and sharing their own. The more he spoke, the more he was understood . . . and the more he understood others.

He was blooming, unbroken forevermore.

Rooted.

⤶ MORAL ⤷

The hurt you hide doesn't disappear—but in time, it may bloom into something that helps you remember how far you've come.

CHAPTER 5

THE CAPYBARA WHO REFUSED THE GATEKEEPER

(For those who've been told they weren't ready, weren't enough, weren't invited)

Capybara arrived at a gate he hadn't known he was walking toward. It was just suddenly there, like a mirage but very real, and he stopped to give the situation further consideration.

The gate hadn't been marked by signs or whispered about in riverside conversations. No map had shown it. No friend had mentioned it. But there it was.

Just a shimmering arch over two large, flat stones,

guarded by four tall cranes with ash-grey feathers and unreadable dark eyes. They wore dark vests and lace-up boots. Their wings were folded tight against their bodies, clutching clipboards and pens at the very tips. Their necks curled like question marks, and they glared at him.

One of them squawked, "You're early."

Another murmured, "You're late."

"You didn't bring the right references," a third chimed in.

"You didn't follow the path," said the last crane. "You weren't cleared."

The capybara blinked. "I-I didn't know . . ."

Without another word, they gave him a scroll, and he released the scarlet cord that bound it. The scroll unfurled, and he spied movement on the page. He looked closer. Lines and cryptic symbols flickered, enlarging then fading away.

Some questions were carved in bark, and the bark itself lifted from the page, as if demanding to be read and answered. Other questions floated past in streams, and he could hear the rushing water. And some were whispered in the wind, in languages he'd never learned to speak.

He tried to understand. He tried to answer. He waited patiently, asked politely, studied quietly. Because that's what he had been taught—to be grateful, to be good, to follow the rules even when no one told him what they were.

He stayed there at the gate for a long while. Scroll in hand, nearly fully unfolded and touching his toes. The shadowy cranes unmoving, though demanding at the same time.

And then, finally, the capybara stopped waiting.

He stepped to the side and simply turned away from the gate. He was not angry, stubborn, or willful.

He was . . . enough. He refused to measure himself by gates he didn't build.

And he reembarked on his journey.

He strolled into the tall grass a few steps down from the gate, where there were no questions—only breeze. He crossed rivers that didn't ask who he was. He found a tree, old and kind, that didn't require a single explanation. He sat there with his back to the trunk, looking up into the vast labyrinth of branches and leaves—opportunities at every turn. He sighed and wiggled up close to the old trunk, and he was certain, nearly certain, he felt its embrace.

In the shade, against the tree, under its maze of limbs and leaves, Capybara remembered something he had always known but simply forgotten.

He belonged in this world. Not because any said it was so, but because he was.

He existed. He lived. He loved. And the parts of the world that truly mattered to him . . . well, they loved him right back.

MORAL

*You don't need permission to exist as you are.
Walk where your heart leads, and the
world will meet you there.*

CHAPTER 6

THE LETTER THE SPIDER SPUN

(For those who are learning to name their own light)

Spider wrote it on a Tuesday in silver thread—the kind spun at first light. It was dewy, and she waited for the sun to dry it.

She detached the threaded message from its holdings, smoothed it flat, and laid it on a rock. She placed another stone atop it, turning it into a one-page book. Then, with care, she slid the entire bundle into a narrow crevice in the old tree—one known only to her. She had cleared it and woven it just for this purpose.

Skittering back a few steps, she viewed her hidey-hole from all angles.

Perfect.

It was meant for someone who might never exist. But she felt compelled to write it anyway. Perhaps her legs needed to say what her voice never could.

The letter began: "To the One Who Sees Me."

And the words that followed were all the things she rarely said aloud about herself.

Intelligent. Gentle. Beautiful in her own quiet way.

Kind. Curious. A little strange. Creative.

And wholly, wonderfully herself.

Time passed. The stone-bound letter gathered dust and dirt, buried by the changing seasons. And Spider forgot about it as she did her spider work.

Until one day, she came across her crevice of secrets once again.

Using a silky rope, she drew the bundle out and removed the top stone . . .

And there it was. The letter. The page of white silk—delicate, yet strong.

Like the letter, she was older now too, softer around the edges. She was tender with her wrinkles and aches and wondering about her future. Where she fit, now that her weaving had slowed and most of her life hung behind her. If she even mattered.

She skittered closer and read the letter.

And the wind grew stronger around her, ruffling the fine hairs on her legs and whispering: "I see you now."

Spider wept like she had back then, when she'd first spun it. But this time, she let the tears fall without hiding them.

Because she realized . . . maybe the One Who Sees her wasn't out there.

Maybe the One had always been herself, the spider holding the letter.

MORAL

Sometimes the love we wait for is the love we were always meant to give ourselves.

CHAPTER 7

THE DOG WHO TRIED TOO HARD

(For those who try to be good so they won't be left behind)

e was the best boy.

Dog was loyal, quiet, and careful. He wagged his tail, even when he didn't feel like it so much. He followed, even when he was tired. He obeyed . . . because that's what good dogs do.

And for a while, being good felt good.

But over time, the praise felt thinner. The smiles stopped reaching him. The rules got heavier. Sit. Stay. Quiet. Not now.

Still, he tried.

He tried until his tail drooped, until he stopped

chasing butterflies, until he forgot the feeling of rolling belly-up in the grass just because it felt good.

One day, Dog curled up under the porch, closed his eyes, and dreamed of a time when being a dog didn't mean being perfect. Just present.

When he woke, he remembered the dream and was filled with an awareness he hadn't had before. This time, he didn't rush to please. He didn't wait to be called.

Instead, he wandered. Not to leave . . . but to find.

And what he found was a clearing full of

wildflowers. A breeze that didn't bark orders. A stranger who didn't ask for tricks but just sat quietly beside him.

There, for the first time in a long time, Dog felt seen. Not for what he did, but for who he was. And that was the very nicest feeling of all.

MORAL

The truest love is unconditional. Without it, we shrink. With it, we grow into our fullest, brightest selves.

CHAPTER 8

THE WOLF WHO LEFT THE PACK

*(For those who must walk away
to become whole)*

er howl mostly went unechoed in the canyons, drowned out by others who were louder and more demanding, forever chasing greatness.

Wolf stayed with the pack, curling her body small so the others wouldn't think she wanted too much. They'd said that before—that she was selfish for needing space, or even for needing them. That she was ungrateful for asking questions. Difficult for needing to understand.

She nodded and followed and soon forgot the sound of her own footsteps.

Seasons passed, her life quietly fading into lonely rhythms, while others in the pack dazzled—too busy shining to see her dim.

Late one evening, Wolf found herself walking away from the pack, and no one came after her. Perhaps they hadn't noticed. She was alone for real this time. At first it stung—being forgotten.

But the air was cleaner without their rules.

The moon was brighter, and she slept under stars that soothed her, and she listened to the wind that shared its knowledge. She became sleeker and wiser and breathed more freely without the weight of their expectations.

Okay, maybe she missed the warmth of bodies beside her. But she did not miss the coldness that came with being invisible within the crowd.

Weeks passed. And the wild became her.

On one thrilling night, when the moon was high in the sky, she lifted her head and howled. The deep, rich sound echoed back to her, wrapping her in its truth. She howled again and again.

Not to be heard by anyone else, but more because she enjoyed hearing the sound of her own voice, finally. It returned to her each time, just as it should have all along, and she wept gratefully.

Then . . . far, far away, she heard a single howl rise in answer. Not from her old pack, but from one she had yet to meet.

MORAL

Sometimes, walking away isn't the end of the story.
It's the beginning of coming home to yourself—
and calling in the ones who see you clearly.

CHAPTER 9

THE ONE INSIDE THE COCOON

(For those who need to pause until they feel safe to emerge)

Pupa had no wings yet, and that was fine.

Inside the cocoon, the light was soft.

White and silver spindle silk.

Quiet.

Woven with stillness.

Outside was dark.

Not evil.

Not violent.

Just unknown.

And it was not for her—not yet.

Leaning against the wall of softness, Pupa sat

tucked into herself, holding the story she wasn't done living. She didn't try to read quickly. Refused to rush it.

The world outside pressed sometimes.

"Why are you still in there?"

"Haven't you healed yet?"

"Aren't you bored of waiting?"

But she didn't answer. She just turned the page.

She was not afraid. Or stuck. Or worried. Or weird.

She was becoming.

And becoming required time and stillness and

silence that not everyone understood. She stayed in her cocoon, not hidden—but held.

And when the time came, she didn't burst out with a flurry of hey-how-do-you-dos and look-at-me-nows.

She simply opened the threaded wall, stepped into the waiting dark, and brought the light with her.

 MORAL

*The walk toward wholeness doesn't
need an audience. Only readiness.*

CHAPTER 10

THE BEAR WHO RAISED DAUGHTERS

(For those who give freely, protect fiercely
—and still stay soft)

ama Bear never truly slept.

Each winter, she curled into her cave, as all bears do, but her mind stayed wide awake.

She had raised two daughters— fierce, radiant things with wild hearts and their own kind of growl.

One was Sea Glass, shaped by tides and time, resilient in the face of storms.

The other was Wildflower, stubborn and bright, blooming in places no one thought life could grow.

They were loud, and curious, and endlessly hungry for her attention, her answers, her everything.

And Bear gave it. All of it. She gave her days to teaching them to fish, to climb, to stand tall. She gave her nights to watching over them as they dreamed unafraid.

She loved them with the ache of someone who holds up the sky so her children never learn the weight of it.

But in the quiet winters—when the forest fell

silent and the wind whispered *rest*—she found she didn't know how.

She lay in the dark and thought about who she used to be . . .

before the cubs,

before the noise,

before she forgot the cub she used to be, with dreams and needs of her own.

Still, she didn't regret it. Not a breath of it. Only that she lost herself so completely in the giving.

One early spring, before the snow had fully melted, she heard laughter outside the cave.

Her daughters! They'd come home.

Grown now.

Strong.

Brave.

Brilliant.

She placed a paw to her heart, her brown eyes glimmering, and listened.

They didn't call her out of the cave.

They just stayed close. Built a fire.

Shared stories.

And Bear realized something quietly true: *They are no longer mine to shape.*

They are mine to witness.

And what a gift it was to have raised daughters who roamed the forest boldly but still returned to sit by their mother's side when the world asked too much of her.

That day, for the first time in many winters, Bear closed her eyes and slept.

❧ MORAL ☙

Rest comes easiest when love comes full circle.

CHAPTER 11

THE LION WHO DIDN'T ASK PERMISSION

(For those who lead with fire and heart)

She was born starkly golden, and the world kept trying to dim her.

"Be softer," they said.

"Be less."

"Don't take up so much space."

Lion, she of great mane and wisdom, heard them loud and clear, but she refused to shrink. She was power and fire and heart.

Her voice was honey laced with thunder.

Her eyes saw through lies and straight into possibility.

She loved hard and protected fiercely.

When she walked into a room, it changed shape.

Lion wasn't cruel. Or loud just to be loud. She didn't wait to be invited. She became the invitation.

And others followed—not because they were told to follow, but because something in her reminded them of the power they had forgotten, a power they, too, carried.

She roared when it mattered. She rested when she needed. And when she looked you in the eye, you felt it:

"You are not small," she would tell them. "You are not broken. I see you. Now go."

And so Lion led—not by asking, but by being . . . and by roaring only when it truly mattered.

⚜ MORAL ⚜

True power is quiet intention. It steadies the room and gives others permission to rise.

CHAPTER 12

THE OWL AT THE CROSSROADS

(For those who are ready to reclaim their wisdom)

wl stood at the crossroads, surrounded by what had been, what
could be, and what still waited.

Behind her, a broken cocoon. Not
discarded, but transformed, standing
tall like a door she'd just walked
through.

Over her left shoulder, two figures lingered—one
with silver eyes, the other with hands worn like river
stones. They did not speak. They didn't need to. She
heard them just fine.

To her right, a swirling, horrible force clawed at the air—a monster made of fear and past noise. It pulled at her feathers and howled and begged her to fall back in. She quickly turned away.

To her left, a house with a wide porch and open gate. Children laughed as they played. Animals bounded through the grass. It smelled like warm bread and a life she believed in.

And straight ahead—a tunnel. Dark, narrow, endless.

Hesitating, Owl glanced back at her guides. They did not move. Not to push her or pull her. She realized they were there to stand with her. What came next was her own.

The vortex shrieked her name, its shadows lapping at her, trying to draw her in.

She covered her eyes with her wings and whispered, "No." She turned to face the monster and said it again, louder, "No!"

The wind shifted, and the dark vortex began to lose its power.

Shrinking.

Fading.

Vanishing like mist.

The tunnel ahead suddenly glowed with light as old sconces flickered to life—one by one by one . . .

Stone shelves lined the walls.

Ancient tomes lined the shelves.

Thousands. Millions. More than time could hold.

Owl flew to the entrance. Landed softly. Her talons silent on the earth floor.

Each book whispered a name, a lifetime, a lesson.

But without guilt or shame. Just truths. Awesome, magical truths.

She reached for a spine—the leather soft, the pages worn from memory.

"Welcome," it said, like she was familiar.

And she was. This was her history and her future in this tunnel. She was finally ready to remember what she had always known.

MORAL

The path to becoming is not found—
it is remembered.

ANIMAL & ELEMENT SYMBOLISM GLOSSARY

These fables live in the realm of symbol, not science. A lion may wear a mane and still be she. The orca—often called a killer whale, though truly a dolphin—still carries the ocean's song. Each animal here is chosen for who it represents, not for taxonomy, but for truth of the heart.

These are not just animals or things.
They are messengers.
They are memory.
Each one appeared in a fable in this book, but they walk beside us still . . . if you let them.

Red Fox
Forward Grace · Self-reclamation
Repatterning

Fox carried what was long after it had lightened—out of love, out of memory, out of habit. She teaches us that letting go isn't forgetting; it's choosing what to carry next. Not for others, but for yourself.

"For the first time, she wondered what she might want to carry next—not for someone else, but for herself."

Whale
Deep Emotion · Ancestral Memory
Healing Through Release

The whale holds what others can't bear. She swallows sorrow and keeps swimming—but when she sings, the ocean listens. Her voice teaches that release is a kind of wisdom, and witnessing is a kind of love.

"The sorrow spilled out of her, not in pieces, but in waves."

Oak Tree

Grounded Wisdom · Inner
Knowing · Ancestral Strength
Soul Alignment · Refuge

The oak is a keeper of ancient truths. She does not sway to be liked or bend to be praised. Her strength is rooted in deep purpose—in the soul line that connects her to all who came before.

"And the storm broke around her. Not through her. Not under her. Around her."

Turtle

Patience · Ancient Wisdom
Inner Timing

The turtle reminds us that holding pain does not make us weak—it makes us human. He teaches us that scars can soften over time, and from the quietest places, beauty may bloom.

"He began to speak, not to explain the pain so much, but to honor the wounds that had nurtured the blooms."

Stag

Guidance · Protection
Threshold Walker

The stag is the presence we feel but can't name—the one who shows up when we are ready to rise. He does not push. He simply appears and supports.

*"These are beautiful. Oh, what you must have
endured to grow them."*

Capybara

Quiet Strength · Self-Worth
Grounded Rebellion · Belonging

The capybara is the calm in a chaotic world—a creature who doesn't rush, compete, or perform to earn space. He reminds us that presence is power.

*"He refused to measure himself by
gates he didn't build."*

Spider

Sacred Expression · Quiet Truth
Creation as Healing

The spider weaves not to capture, but to remember—
each thread a truth too heavy to carry inside. She
reminds us that what we create in silence still
matters.

"Perhaps her legs needed to say
what her voice never could."

Dog

Loyalty · Service
Devotion

The faithful one who follows, serves, and waits . . .
but also needs time to play. Dog reminds us that
devotion is noble, but not if it costs your wholeness.

"Dog curled up under the porch and dreamed of a time
when being a dog didn't mean being perfect."

Wolf
Instinct · Honoring Self
Reverent Solitude · Freedom

The wolf left the pack—not in rebellion, but in truth. Her fable belongs to those who've been silenced by belonging and healed by walking alone.

"She howled again and again. Not to be heard by anyone else—more because she enjoyed hearing the sound of her own voice, finally."

Pupa / Butterfly
Transformation · Divine Timing
Rebirth

The butterfly didn't rush. She honored the pause. Her cocoon was not a prison, but a womb.

"She was not afraid. Or stuck. Or worried. Or weird. She was becoming."

Bear

Quiet Strength
Devotional Mothering
The Matriarch's Pause

The bear isn't really sleeping; she's pretending. Her fable reminds us that not all stillness is restful, but even a tired heart can trust the harvest to come . . . then rest and rejoice.

"They are no longer mine to shape.
They are mine to witness."

Sea Glass

Transformation · Softness Through
Struggle · Soul Weathering

Sea glass is what happens when something broken refuses to stay sharp. It returns with gentler edges— and a shimmer that wasn't there before.

"One was Sea Glass, shaped by tides and time,
resilient in the face of storms."

Wildflower

Resilience · Beauty in the Margins
Rooted Bravery

Wildflowers bloom where no one expects them to—sidewalk cracks, dry ditches, broken earth. They don't ask. They just grow.

"The other was Wildflower, stubborn and bright, blooming in places no one thought life could grow."

Lion

Embodied Strength · Leadership
Protective Truth

The lion doesn't wait to be asked. She leads with fire and steadiness, teaching that love is not weakness—it is power with purpose.

"She didn't wait to be invited.
She became the invitation."

Owl

Wisdom · Thresholds
Spiritual Sight · Reclamation

The owl waits until the moment is true. She stands at the crossroads not with fear, but with remembering.

*"She was finally ready to remember
what she had always known."*

RITUALS FOR AFFIRMATION, ABUNDANCE, AND HEALING

These practices are meant to comfort and inspire. They are not prescriptive or diagnostic, but rather gentle invitations to reconnect with yourself. You don't need to believe in "magic" for them to work. Please honor what feels true for you and release the rest.

Each is connected to one or more of the fables. Let them meet you where you are. Let them move through your hands, your breath, your words.

Water Ritual
"THE LETTING FLOW"

For when you feel emotionally stuck or full of old grief

What you'll need: A bowl of water or access to a stream, tub, or sink. Optional: sea salt or flower petals.

Steps:

1. Pour the water with care—like you're preparing a sacred space.
2. Hold your hands above it and say: "I am allowed to soften. I am allowed to let go. I do not have to hold it all."
3. Dip your hands in the water. Let the water carry what you're ready to release.
4. Pour the water out slowly—into the earth or down the drain—whispering: *"I carry it no more, but I honor where it brought me."*

Gardening Ritual
"THE SEED OF AWAKENING"

*For when you are starting over, planting truth,
or reclaiming your ground*

What you'll need: A seed, a small plant, or even a stone. A space to place it.

Steps:
1. Hold your object. Speak a word you want to grow: trust, courage, home, voice . . .
2. Place it into soil or on your altar and say: "I plant this not to rush it, but to remember that I grow too."
3. Tend to it as you would yourself. Slowly. Gently. As needed.

Breath Ritual
"THE SOFT RETURN"

For when you feel scattered, anxious, or overextended

What you'll need: Just your breath and a quiet space

Steps:
1. Hand over heart. Inhale deeply. Exhale slowly.
2. Imagine your energy returning to you on every breath out.
3. Whisper: "I am not scattered. I return to myself now."
4. After a few rounds, softly affirm: "I am still here. I am whole."

Sound Ritual

"The Resonant Thread"

*For when a fable stirred something in you
that's still unnamed*

What you'll need: One piece of music that moves you

Steps:

1. Sit or lie down. Press play with intention.
2. Let the music thread through your body. No need to understand—just feel.
3. When it ends, whisper the one truth that's present in you now.
4. Optional: Write it down. Tuck it into this book.

Burn and Release Ritual

"THE CLEARING"

For when you're carrying stories, dreams, or emotions that no longer belong to you

What you'll need: Paper and pen

Steps:

1. Write how something made you feel—don't tell the story, just the feeling.
2. Fold the paper. Say: "Thank you for teaching me. I release you."
3. Burn it safely, or tear and bury it.
4. Whisper one or more of the following:
   a. "I choose truth. I choose peace."
   b. "I release what still tries to please, escape, or prove."
   c. "I choose to become."
5. Wash your hands. Drink water. Place your hand on your heart and say, *"I am safe in my unfolding."*

Inner Child Ritual
"THE REMEMBERING"

*For when you feel triggered, abandoned,
or unsure of your worth*

What you'll need: Your own voice

Steps:

1. Begin by saying aloud: "Dear younger me . . ." or "To the part of me who still feels trapped . . ."
2. Speak freely. Let the words rise. You might say:
    a. "I see now how much you carried."
    b. "They told you to be good. You tried so hard."
    c. "But you don't owe them a life that isn't yours."
    d. "I'm here now. I see you. You're not alone."
3. Close with: "You can rest now. I've got us from here."

DECLARATION OF BECOMING

A personal invocation for the unfinished soul.

I am no longer the person who was handed off.
No longer the one who said yes to things they
didn't want
just to keep the peace.
Just to be loved.
Just to be "good."

I am not here to pass anyone's test.
Not the ones created by systems.
Not the ones written by guardians.
Not even the ones I wrote myself
when I was too young to know better.

I do not owe my joy to those who praised
my obedience.
I do not owe my life to those who made me shrink.
I do not owe my voice to silence.

I release clothes that don't fit, the old roles,
the shrinking spaces.
I choose expansion.
I choose rootedness.
I choose me.

I will build my own wings.
If I knock down the gate.
If I must walk alone for a while,
let it be the most honest walk I've ever taken.
I am not trapped.
I am transforming.
Not everyone will understand.
But I do.
And I will never forget again.

I do not have to pass a test to be worthy of joy.
I do not have to carry others' expectations
in order to be good.
I release the old patterns that kept me small.

I honor who I was, who I am, and who
I am becoming.
I am not stuck. I am in motion.
I am not lost. I am unfolding.
I do not need permission. I am already enough.
I'm stepping into my next self. And I am
ready for me.

AUTHOR'S NOTE

How This Book Found Me

This book wasn't planned. It arrived like a whisper, rising up from all around me like something that had always been there, just waiting to be noticed, really. It became a thread I kept tugging at until it unraveled into something whole. It came in the in-between spaces: insomnia and morning meditations, the pauses during daily routines, and the truths that come from connection, not just conversation.

And there was reiki. In those quietly electric sessions—guided by my youngest daughter, a gentle and gifted healer—I began to remember who I was before I forgot. I saw myself on a flying carpet, wild with joy. I sat inside a silvery cocoon, reading and waiting for safety to return. I stood at the threshold of a dark tunnel that transformed, lantern by lantern, into a library filled with my soul line . . . the stories and truths I carry, and those that carry me.

I also began to see with new eyes through my oldest daughter, whose fierce spirit mirrors my own. When I asked forgiveness for my youthful naivety as a mother, she offered it with grace. Our reconnection became one of my life's great gifts, and in it, I was reminded that becoming doesn't always mean moving forward—sometimes, it means turning around and opening my arms.

This book was also stirred by dreams. The kind that don't fade with morning. Dreams that carried emotion I couldn't shake, images I didn't fully understand . . . people I longed for, paths I never took, doors that didn't open when they should have. These visions stirred something old in me, something that had been waiting patiently to be named.

What else could I do but write?

The fables came during a shift I took with intention—between old chapters and new beginnings, which I am experiencing now in both vivid color and subtle shadow. They came from the unfinished parts of me. And I am learning to love those parts most of all; they remind me I'm still growing and glowing. And that means I'm alive.

My soul circle—a small group of men and women who have lifted me and opened my heart in ways I never could have imagined—are the catalysts behind these new insights that have changed me. I am softer, but also stronger. I see the world so differently now. And when I think of how many may never know what it is to feel safe enough to soften ... well, I can hardly bear the thought.

Again, what else could I do but write?

So I offer these fables to you. May they meet you in your own moment of unfolding and self-recognition.

These are the ships we sail ... fables built not for answers, but for the brave act of becoming.

A GENTLE NOTE FOR YOUR VOYAGE

If something stirred in you—a memory, a question, a truth you didn't expect to meet here—don't rush to explain it. Just notice. Let it walk beside you a while. Let it speak when it's ready.

And when *you're* ready, take it to a place that belongs to you.

Not this book. *Yours.* A journal. A piece of paper. The back of an envelope. A whisper in the dark that you vow not to forget.

Write it down. Not to fix it. Not to name it perfectly. But to make space for whatever part of you has been waiting to be seen.

This book is only one companion.

You are the real story.

From my heart to yours—
THANK YOU
for reading *The Ships We Sail*.

My hope is that these fables offered stillness, inspiration, or simply a reminder that you are exactly where you're meant to be. If they did, would you share your thoughts in a review on Amazon or your favorite bookseller's site? Your words are a gift to future readers who may need this book, too.

Amazon Link/ QR Code:
https://amzn.to/3K5uQqJ

ABOUT THE AUTHOR

Janet Fix is a seasoned publisher, editor, and multi-genre writer whose work spans gripping mysteries, heartwarming children's stories, and soulful modern fables. With decades of publishing experience and global collaborations, Janet balances coaching other authors with her own creative writing.

Outside the world of books, Janet is a passionate researcher, avid gardener, and devoted grandmother to four granddaughters. She finds joy in the exploration of words, the quiet power of manifestation, and the healing energy of nature and intention—helping others find the courage to tell their own stories.

www.janetfix.com

If you'd like to continue this journey together, please subscribe to my newsletter, where I share more uplifting reflections and bookish goodies. I'd love to stay connected.

Link/QR Code:
www.janetfix.com

With gratitude,
—*Janet*

ABOUT
THE COVER ARTIST

Elena Stowell is an award-winning author, illustrator, and passionate Brazilian jiu-jitsu practitioner. When she isn't crafting stories, she's creating mixed-media illustrations, happily surrounded by paper scraps, dried paint, and glue sticks.

Elena is the author of *Flowing with the Go: A Jiu-Jitsu Journey of the Soul*, the children's books *Frango & Chicken* and *The Knotting Tree*, and co-founder of the Carly Stowell Foundation. Through her creative work and volunteer efforts, Elena strives to break down barriers, helping others overcome adversity and find hope through meaningful engagement in sports, music, and art.

www.elenastowell.com

.

www.ingramcontent.com/pod-product-compliance
Lightning Source LLC
Chambersburg PA
CBHW031447120626
46545CB00006B/2597